MW01290535

Book Repair for Booksellers

A handy guide for booksellers and
book collectors offering practical advice
on how to improve the quality and look

of your books and ephemera

by J. Godsey

SicPress 2013
Methuen, Mass

©2009, 2013 J Godsey & SicPress.com
14 Pleasant St.
Methuen, Massachusetts.
sales@sicpress.com

Print Edition
ISBN-10 1442137320
ISBN-13 978-1442137325

Also available in digital format and Kindle edition.

TABLE OF CONTENTS

PREFACE

Book repair for booksellers. Traditionally there are two types of book repair books: those where the end goal is to prepare the book for further intense circulation, and thus aesthetics take a backseat to durability; and those that focus on archival preservation and restoration of books of historical or monetary value. This leaves booksellers wandering in the desert, with a stack of books that aren't valuable enough to send out for professional restoration, yet are too good to discard.

I have seen books repaired with book tape, duct tape, electric tape, and masking tape. I have seen rubber cement, white glue, airplane glue, superglue, and hot glue. I have seen them priced with stickers, ink, crayon, marker, and lipstick. And I have been asked to remove every bit of it. Some of these mutilations were done by people I know and respect in the field. I have even done a few myself: I did library-type repairs on books in high school and have been paying penance ever since.

I know a bookbinder who sells bottles of furniture polish and neatsfoot oil and calls it "book crème." I know another who buys saddle polish and relabels it as a "leather book treatment." And I know a bookstore that uses electrical tape to reback reading copies. There are better and less dangerous methods of repair however that are just as easy.

I will admit that not every book deserves archival quality treatment. That inexpensive copy of a book club bestseller without a dust jacket deserves a spiffy new outlook on life, but not to the extent of spending an hour of my life dry cleaning and redyeing it.

If you have 30 dollars into a 100 dollar book, you don't want to spend another 75 on a full-boat restoration when a 25 buck reback will do. Take the time to learn which books not to harm and you won't have to worry about what happens to a book you sold 40 years down the road.

When should a book be sent out for repairs and when should you work on it yourself?

- If you don't know the book's true value, STOP.

- If you think you may harm it, STOP.

- If you aren't sure what it's going to look like later, STOP.

- If you can't afford to throw it away after you have ruined it, STOP.

Use your head before you use your hands. One can easily turn a good book into scrap paper. It is assumed that you have researched the damaged book and found it not valuable enough to demand repair by a professional. It is more work for the conservator to correct a bad repair than to just start from scratch. If the book has great monetary or sentimental value, it is probably best left "as is" or restored by a professional.

When in doubt: DO NOTHING. Give it a once over for 10 minutes then sell it as is. Doing nothing is the safest course of action. Doing repairs that keep small injuries from becoming big ones is even better.

Respect the book. Don't use products that aren't meant to be used on books, such as superglue, hot glue, epoxy, or duct tape. If you don't respect the integrity of the book, you are in the wrong business. For example, I saw a nice first edition at a book show where the endpapers had been so badly replaced that the book was now practically worthless – since reversing the bad repair would have caused even more damage.

Do what you feel comfortable doing. You can do fixes that can't be reversed on books that are never going to increase in value. But if it may increase in value, don't mess with it unless you know what you are doing. Start small: facelifts, erasing, lifting stickers, tipping in pages, tightening spines. Most importantly, practice new methods first on worthless books, that's what they are for!

Do the math. Book A is worth $25 in GOOD condition. If it needs anything that takes longer than 10 minutes, it is not worth doing. Things you can do in 10 minutes: erasing, remove stickers, surface cleaning, fix tears and loose pages. If you spent 1 hour on it, and you sold it immediately, you won't even be breaking even.

Book B in GOOD condition would bring $75. If it needs a total rebind, it is worthless – give it away. If it merely needs rebacking, but then is worth only a fraction, sell it as is, and let the end user worry about fixing it.

Book C is worth $250 in GOOD condition and you have less than $100 into it already. Do the 10 minute repairs yourself. If it needs a reback and you KNOW how, you can do that. If you are adept at major repairs, you can do them, but remember your TIME is worth something. And most booksellers don't have the TIME to do major repairs themselves. If it needs major repairs and you can't do them, sell it as is, let the customer spend the dough on a repair. Sending it out to be fixed will eat into your profits too much.

Send it out. If the book is worth more than $250, send it to a professional or sell it as is. When you pay for a book to be repaired, you will have to work the costs of the repair into your sale price. If you don't have a ready customer for it, you may have to wait awhile to get that money back. Sometimes forever. Most high end sellers will easily spend money on what needs doing, because once they can display the book, they can generate interest in it. If it is damaged, they can only talk about it.

If you only list on databases and the book will SIT waiting to sell, don't bother, sell it as is. If you have to hang on to it for a year, you have tied your money up paying for something that your customer could have paid for. If someone is interested in it, offer to send it to a binder for them and have them pick up the tab.

Library discards. Most library discards are not valuable; the large percentage are little more than reading copies and cleaned up can serve as very nice shelf copies. A very small percentage are books that are scarce in any condition and with a little bit of careful attention can be greatly enhanced. However, there are a minute number of books that should not be "fixed" by an amateur. It is expected that you have researched your books and know the difference between books you can work on yourself and books you should send to a professional.

Price fairly. For a flawed book, I suggest you do your research and come up with a price you feel comfortable with but can easily get. You will likely only get a fraction of the value of a flawless copy (depending on the rarity of the title). If you hold out for the "best possible price" you will probably end up owning the book for a very, very long time. Don't be greedy, since you don't have a lot of money into the item, just get your money and get out.

Offer it to a few other sellers who carry similar books, and see if they are interested; if they come close to your price, sell it. They know the market better than you do. Don't be surprised, however, if a high end seller isn't interested in a flawed copy – it's nothing personal, it just won't fit into their catalog.

Throw it on an auction site and give the collectors a chance at it. You may do much better, as collectors who can't afford a perfect copy may see yours as a great bargain. You can even sit on the item for awhile; if you only have a few dollars into it, why rush?

Be honest. If you have done anything beyond simple cleaning and erasing, tightening a hinge or tipping in a loose page, list the repair in your description. If a torn page has been repaired and looks just dandy, say it has been "professionally repaired." If the book has been rebacked, rebound or had the endpapers replaced, you must declare it in your description or risk it being returned.

Be patient. Whether you are removing self-adhesive stickers, pre-gummed bookplates, or doing other book fixes, a major factor in a successful fix is time and patience. With all fixes, you need to analyze the situation and test your fixes on similar papers and sacrificial books; this is a step many people skip. Impatience gets people in a lot of tight spots and makes for sloppy results.

Be organized.

1. Group repairs together by difficulty. Do small repairs in batches, and big repairs alone.

2. Set repair projects aside for quiet time, e.g., late night or early morning, weekends, holidays, times when nothing else is demanding your attention.

3. Clear the work area of everything else.

4. Assemble your tools, even ones you may not need.

5. Don't use household tools, have TWO sets, and keep your repair tools in a special box, drawer, or toolbox.

6. Turn on music or an audio book. Turn off the phone.

7. Don't have you drink at hand, put it one step away from your work area.

8. If you have pets or children, secure your work area when you walk away. Close liquids, cover papers.

9. Let things dry at their own pace, which means overnight if need be.

10. When you are finished, clean your tools and put them away.

Toolbox

Parts books. Some books are more valuable for their parts than the whole. An old bookseller's trick is to tear out the free endpapers before discarding the book. I take this one step further: tear out the free endpapers, rip off the boards, remove ribbon markers, plates, even epigraphs or colophons if they only have a single line on them. Once you have harvested the book parts, save the endpapers and blank flyleaves in a one file drawer. Group them by width and height; let the age, color, and material take care of themselves. When trying to match, start with the folder of items nearest the original size and work your way up through the sizes. Remember, large epigraph or dedication pages can be cut down for smaller books.

Tools.

Straight edge. 18" straight edge or metal ruler. A heavy steel right angle is also very useful.

Bone folder. Several shapes: pointy, blunt, thick, thin, long, short. Can be bone, nylon, or Teflon.

Sanding sponges. Commonly used for drywall smoothing, very fine grades are great for cleaning up fore-edges and text blocks.

Brushes. Fat stencil brushes are good for applying large amounts of paste; disposable paint brushes (particularly nylon ones) are good for applying small amounts of glue. Large, fat, soft paint or shoe brushes are good for dusting.

Cotton swabs, balls and cosmetic rounds. All are useful for applying glues, dyes, and solvents.

Paring knife or micro spatula. Both are useful for lifting wet, tiny or gluey stuff.

Plastic spatulas, sticker removers, plastic razor blades. Are all useful for lifting stickers.

Blunt tweezers. The six-inch tweezers sold for handling postage stamps are quite good and cheap.

Large plastic syringes or irrigators. Both are useful for getting glue exactly and precisely where it is wanted.

Utility knife. Knives with snap-off blades are very popular among conservators; scalpels are even better; as are razor or Exacto® blades. Do not reuse dull disposable blades, as they will tear the paper.

Heat source. Quilting, tacking or clothes iron; also helpful are hair driers and small chemical-based heating pads.

Thin dowels. Long 18" metal rods, chopsticks, knitting needles, bamboo skewers. These are used to secure the groove in the shoulder.

Mesh or elastic bandages. Roll type such as Ace® brand, both stretchy and cheesecloth.

C-clamps. Assorted sizes, small ones are very useful, as are ones with deep throats.

Bulldog clips. Large, small, and you can never have too many.

Covered bricks. These substitute for the third hand you don't have. Slide them into tube socks or wrap them like a present with book cloth, vinyl, oil cloth, or duck. Fire bricks are much heavier than ordinary bricks.

Copy or book binding press. In a perfect world, we would all have a 19th century cast iron copy press handy, but odd encyclopedia volumes, heavy art books, or piles of bricks will suffice.

Laying press. If you can't afford a proper one, devise something from hardwoods and threaded rods that will hold a book tightly with the spine facing up.

Masonite boards. Very useful for holding a text block tightly, either with C-clamps or in a laying press. Thin and strong, can be found at art supply stores.

SUPPLIES

PVA (polyvinyl acetate). pH neutral PVA should be thinned a bit with water, wheat paste or methyl cellulose before using. A 50/50 blend of PVA and methyl cellulose is a common adhesive. In a pinch I use wallpaper paste; mixed much thinner and smoother than normal, it works very well. Household white glue is OVA but it is not pH neutral for general book work.

Protective sheeting. Wax paper, plastic bags, polyethylene, Mylar film, baking parchment, silicon release paper.

Absorbent paper. Blotter paper or watercolor paper. Water and paper don't mix. The only way to get it out at home without causing a warp is to suck it out under weight or iron it dry.

Copy paper. General cheap computer paper is useful for covering work surfaces, dabbing glue brushes onto.

Mending tissue. Thin and medium weight Japanese tissues; lightweight for paper tears, medium weight for hinge repairs.

Document repair tape. Archival repair tape provides quick, safe repairs or stabilization for torn art, books, or documents. Uses a strong, very thin, acid-free tissue coated with neutral pH self-stick adhesive. When applied, the tape virtually disappears to give an unobtrusive and safe repair. While the repair is generally considered permanent, the tape can be removed with mineral spirits if desired. Two widths, 1/2" and 1" are available.

Polybags. Clean, brand new polybags in various sizes. Storing damaged books in individual bags prevents the damaged from becoming worse and keeps all the parts together.

Index cards. Index cards are the ideal tool to notate a book's history and future needs. Acquisition date, present condition, detailed damages, and repair requirements.

Solvents. There are many solvents on the market; most are hazardous to your health and some are hazardous to books. Commonly available products that include naphtha and heptane as their active ingredient will evaporate 100% and should be sufficient for most bookseller needs. Many professional strength products are overkill when your aim is merely to remove a sticker. Make sure to have adequate ventilation when using solvents and wear gloves/protective eyewear.

Ronsonol® lighter fluid = Naphtha

Un-Du® = 100% Heptane

Bestine® rubber cement thinner = 100% Heptane

Blaster® E-Z Take away = Mineral Spirits and Isopropyl (Propane)

Goo Gone® = Naphtha with added Citrus Oil , citrus oil should not be used near paper as it does not evaporate.

Goof off® = Xylene and Methanol. Xylene is too strong to use on books and will remove the inks and coatings from dust jackets.

Other Products. These are generally optional, but as they are referenced in various solutions, below is an all-in-one list. The characteristics and use of each product are described under the appropriate solution. Supplier information is listed at the end of the book.

Absorene ®. Dry book/paper cleaner.

Sterling's Magic®. Dry book/paper cleaner.

Clean Cover Ge®l: Wet, no-water book cover cleaner.

Lexol pH®: Leather cleaner.

British Museum Formula: Leather protectant.

Triple Crown Dressing (Fredelka)®: Leather protectant.

Klucel-G: Leather consolidant (red rot treatment) in raw powdered form.

Cellugel®: Leather consolidant pre-mixed with anhydrous alcohol.

Meltonian Shoe Cream®: Conditions and enhances the color of leather.

ERASERS

Vinyl. The most popular type of eraser, they have a plastic-like texture and erase more cleanly than other types. They tend to be softer and non-abrasive, making them less likely to damage canvas or paper. However, vinyl erasers can range from very soft and malleable to firm and unyielding. The firmer the eraser, the more prone it is to smearing when erasing large areas or dark marks. Because of its natural tendency to adhere graphite and dirt to itself, vinyl are ideal all-purpose erasers. Found in assorted shapes and sizes, for book work the standard small rectangle is favored, and the "stick" shape in a plastic pencil holder is an ideal companion. New ergonomic shapes, such as ovoid and triangular, are very popular for people who do a lot of erasing.

Gum. Traditionally made from natural gums and resins, these are now more commonly being made with soy resins. Because of its crumbly nature, the art gum eraser is a favorite for cleaning large sections of fingerprints and smudges. The dirt adheres to the crumbs, which are blown or brushed from the surface. Gum erasers are also available with silica grit added to give the eraser an added gentle abrasion that will remove darker markings and ink from thicker surfaces, such as book paper.

Rubber. With products trending toward "latex free," these are rarely found in natural rubber and are more commonly made from less expensive synthetic rubber. Rubber erasers are firmer and more abrasive than vinyl erasers. They are popular with some booksellers for casual use but not for large clean up. Rubber erasers are prone to smearing, as the graphite adhering to the surface will readily be transferred back to the original surface.

14

Because of its less smooth surface, rubber is also capable of damaging surfaces such as onion skin and coated paper.

Grated eraser. Grated vinyl or gum eraser is an ideal gentle cleaning product. Used extensively by conservators, it can be bought pre-ground in assorted sizes or can be made at home with a cheese grater or coffee grinder. Keeping a mini garlic grater in the drawer with the erasers is very convenient. The granules are sprinkled on the surface of a print or page and gently rolled back and forth under the fingers over small sections at a time. This is all that is needed to cause the dirt particulates to adhere to the eraser bits. Afterward, the eraser granules are blown or brushed away. There are people who have a preference for Sanford Magic rub or Staedtler Mars erasers ground up, but for bookseller purposes there is almost no difference, save that Magic Rubs are cheaper. Erasers too finely ground can become embedded in the weave of the paper or book cloth, too coarsely ground and they won't work well.

Document cleaning pads. These are rosin-type bags filled with eraser particles. If you cut several different ones open, you will most likely find they are all filled with the same thing. The bags are squeezed over the work surface, so that the smallest grains sprinkle down. They can then be worked with the fingertips or even with the bag itself, however ,the latter may provide too much pressure and cause the dirt to work into the item, as well as getting the bag dirty.

Electric erasers. Electric erasers are ideal for rehabilitating textbooks and children's' books. Any place where there are large swatches of underlining or handwriting that need to be erased but not a lot of time to do it in.

Battery powered erasers don't have a lot of torque and the smaller they are the shorter their lifespan. Because of their lack of torque you can't apply much pressure before they stop spinning. This makes them ideal for lighter hand work or for people with limited dexterity. Their drawback is that they take short white vinyl cartridges and burn out and melt at high speeds. They are not recommended for extended use.

Plug-in professional erasers have a lot of torque and are hard to kill, but they can be too powerful for delicate work. Plug in model cartridges are available in three types: white plastic, pink rubber, and gray rubber. All of them work on pencil and grime, though none of them work on ink: one would have to apply too much torque and by then you will have made a hole in the page.

BOOK ANATOMY

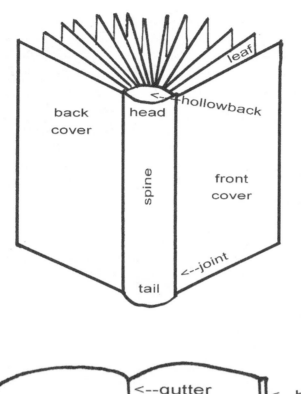

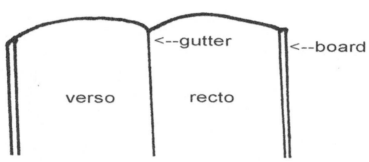

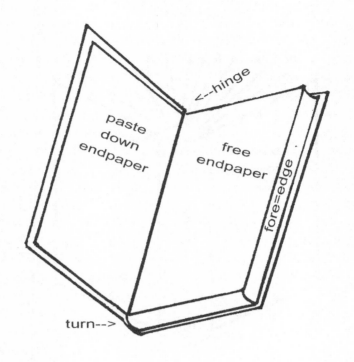

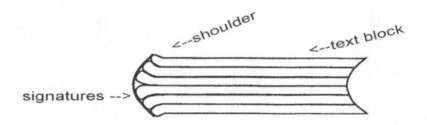

Exterior

Dirty Book

Problem: The exterior of the book has become soiled or dusty. Books should be cleaned and dusted several times a year to prevent dirt from becoming embedded in the surface. The texture of book cloth and leather can retain particulates for decades, even centuries; prolonged handling in this condition can embed the dirt even further. Older books with light colored cloth or wrappers may have foxing, a brown chemical discoloration that cannot be removed by surface cleaning.

Solution A: Lightly go over the book's exterior with a pre-treated dusting cloth.

Solution B: Dust with a soft bristled brush, such as a shoe brush or large paint brush. Hold the book tightly closed, with the spine toward you, and dust the text block and fore-edges away from you.

Solution C: Go over the surface with a micro-pore 100% rubber 'dry cleaning' sponge.

Solution D: Use a series of erasers to go over small sections of dirt. Begin with a white vinyl eraser, and move up to pink rubber, art gum or ink erasers as needed.

Solution E: Use a document cleaning product such as Absorene®; which can be crumbled into fine bits and rubbed against the dirty surface or lightly dabbed on the surface to adsorb the dirt.

Solution F: Use Clean Cover Gel to clean the entire surface equally. Book cloth is NOT color fast, and water-based solutions will cause colors to run, stain, or fade. Clean Cover Gel is not water based and will not cause dyes to run. (It can however sometimes remove a little color from cloth, so make sure to apply evenly to minimize any lightening.) Clean Cover

Gel works well on cloth and softcover books but may have a drying effect on leather.

Solution G: Try dry cleaning fluid or non-water based spot remover on small food and grease stains on book cloth. Spot removers will not work on softcover and leather items may become stained.

Solution H: Use Sterling's Magic to clean the entire surface equally. Sterling's Magic is a pH neutral but water-based cleaner. Book cloth color may run somewhat; however, if it is applied evenly permanent discoloration can be avoided. Sterling's Magic works well on grimy paperback wrappers, and smooth newish leather such as bibles; it should not be used on dried or soft leathers.

Leather Treatment

Problem: Traditionally, leather bindings would stay supple over time from handling, as the natural oils in the hands would keep the leather soft. Leather books are no longer handled, they are shelved and meant to be seen and not touched. Improperly shelved leather books will become dry, cracked, and dirty over time. There is much debate among conservators and antiquarians regarding the chemical compounds recommended for treating leather. However, since we are dealing with relatively inexpensive trade volumes and not those requiring the attentions of a conservator, we can rely on traditional ingredients without causing an international incident.

Note: When working with leather books and oily fluids, wrapping the text block with a sheet of paper is recommended. (see **Text Block Wrap**).

Dirty Leather

Solution A: Saddle soaps that only contain neatsfoot oil, glycerin, and lanolin are rare. These days they also include detergents which over time do more harm than good. If it is a handmade high-end saddle soap, it is probably suitable to clean leather books. All saddle soap containers declare it suitable for books even if it isn't.

Solution B: Lexol pH is a pH-negative, glycerin-based leather cleaner suitable for cleaning book leather.

New-Looking Leather

Solution A: Dust at least twice a year if stored on open shelves, in closed shelves dust once a year.

Solution B: Wipe with a leather protectant formula such as the British Museum formula vended by Talas, which neutralizes acids on the surface, replaces natural salts, and protects against mold and mildew.

DRY LEATHER

Solution A: Rehydrate the leather. If leather is extremely dry, treat with a leather conditioner first; if only merely dry, lubricate with standard leather dressing such as the commonly used New York Public Library recipe of a 60/40 blend of lanolin and neatsfoot oil, vended by Talas and Sicpress.

Solution B: Protect the leather. Triple Crown Leather Dressing (was Fredelka Formula) made by Accessible Archives is an example of a wax-based leather dressing. A blend of neatsfoot oil, beeswax and microwax, the cream adheres to the surface of the leather, allowing the oils to penetrate and the waxes to harden and protect from further damage.

LEATHER RED ROT

Problem: Old leather is high in tannins and is prone to rotting and turning into so much red dust.

Solution. Red rot cannot be reversed; however, with the application of hydroxypropylcellulose the leather can be consoli-

21

dated and the rot can be stopped. Hydroxypropylcellulose is available in two forms: as a powder (marketed as Klucel-G) which has to be blended with a liquid to be applied (usually alcohol), or as a premixed product made from alcohol and Klucel-G, marketed as Cellugel.

1. If using the powder, mix 1 teaspoon of Klucel-G in 1 cup anhydrous alcohol and allow it to sit overnight. Many users have had success using an isopropyl alcohol with a high alcohol content, 85%-95%, such as ethanol or wood grain alcohol. Vodka may have impurities added to it.

2. Wrap the text block to protect it. The mixture will not harm paper-covered boards or labels, but the red rot dust will stain.

3. Using a soft brush, apply a thin coat of prepared Klucel-G or Cellugel to the binding, making certain to get the turn-ins and board edges.

4. Stand the book up with covers splayed open; they should dry quickly. To prevent further damage, a polyester book cover should be made for the book

Dirty Vellum

Problem: Vellum covered book is dirty. Vellum is a stretched and scraped animal skin, used for documents and bookbinding. Constant handling was intended to keep the vellum supple through transfers of oils from the hands to the leather. Vellum will dry out when stored improperly and is especially vulnerable to picking up dirt and grime. Dry vellum should be handled with care and cleaned as delicately as possible.

Solution A: Saliva is the tried and true recommended cleaner for vellum. Spit on a cotton ball or cotton swab and tackle the dirty spots in a small round motion. This should loosen it up and clean it as delicately as possible.

Solution B: Surface dirt can be removed with document cleaning pads or coarsely ground erasers such as Sanford's Magic Rub or Staedtler Mars Plastic eraser. Extremely fine grinds may get stuck in the pores of the vellum.

Solution C: After removing the surface dirt, stains usually remain. A mild liquid leather cleaner such as Lexol-pH can be tried, but this would be overkill for spot cleaning. I would only go that far if you were washing the entire binding.

DIRTY TEXT BLOCK EDGES

Problem: The edges of the text block are not the normal color; usually from being stored in an excessively dirty location.

Solution A: Brush with a soft yet fat brush: shoe brushes, stencil brushes, and extra large paint brushes work very well. Hold the book tightly closed and with the spine toward you and brush away from you, turning the book.

Solution B: Erasers work very well for removing soil and fingerprints from text block edges. Grip the book tightly while holding it against a flat surface, and erase small sections at a time.

Solution C: White edges can be "cleaned" with a sanding sponge, which will conform to its curvature. Grip the text block tightly or put the text block between two pieces of cardboard held together by a c-clamp. Fold the boards back to protect them from harm. Lightly sand the text block edge away from the book in long clean strokes. Sanding sponges (or sanding sheets) can be cut down to just the width you need for a particular text block.

Deckle edges. Some edges are unevenly trimmed; this is called a deckle edge and is not a flaw. Traditionally, the ragged edge indicated handmade paper, now it is deliberately "shaped" during the binding process to be reminiscent of handmade paper. Stiffer bristles may be required to clean deckle edges, such as a clean toothbrush or a nylon bristle brush.

Dyed ("stained") edges. Some edges are dyed (referred to in the trade as "staining") or decorated and will not respond well to abrasion; even direct erasing with a pencil eraser may loosen the color. These should only be cleaned with soft brushes.

Gilt edges. Gilt edges and tooling should be cleaned with a soft cloth or very fine paintbrush. There are "gilt polishing" products on the market, but they are targeted at the antique market and I am not certain how they would affect text blocks. Firmly secure the text block between cardboard and c-clamps before anything at all is applied.

DIRTY DUST JACKET

Problem: The dust jacket has surface dirt.

GLOSSY DUST JACKET

Solution A: A solution of 50% water and 50% all-purpose cleaner, such as Windex®, 409® or Lysol®, applied with a clean cotton rag. Do not spray the jacket directly, as it will soak through.

Solution B: Use a cotton ball and a light application of lighter fluid (naphtha) or a sticker removing product such as Bestine Solvent or Undu. Goo Gone, and other citrus oil solvents can be used if care is taken not to touch the non glossy areas. Goof-Off and other harsh solvents should not be used, as they will eat the coated surface and remove the inks.

MATTE FINISH DUST JACKET OR PRINTS

Solution A: Start with small areas and go over the entire surface with a soft white vinyl eraser.

Solution B: Use a document cleaning bag, and sprinkling minute particles over one area at a time, gently rub these grains over the surface. Follow up by blowing or lightly brushing the residue away with a soft brush.

Solution C: Make your own document cleaning bag/eraser crumbs by finely shredding an art gum or white vinyl eraser with a cheese grater. Sprinkle the particles over one area at a time, gently rub these grains over the surface, follow up by blowing or lightly brushing the residue away with a soft brush.

Solution D: use Absorene® and sprinkle the particles onto the dust jacket surface, then lightly rub/roll the pieces back and forth over the dirty parts, applying just enough pressure to cause some friction. Blow or brush the particles off the surface. Repeat with clean particles.

WRINKLED DUST JACKET

Problem: There is a fold, wrinkle, or wave in the dust jacket.

Solution:

1. Remove the dust jacket from the book

2. Put it face down on a smooth heat-proof surface like a kitchen counter. If you put it face up, you may impress the texture of the towel into the coated surface.

3. Put a smooth non-fluffy dish towel over it.

4. Iron it with a clothes iron on low. For a fold, use an iron with a small head to direct the head, such as a quilting iron.

5. Let it cool before you remove it from the surface, peeling it up while warm can cause curling.

Augmentation

Stickers and Tape

Problem: Something has been stuck to the board, dust jacket, or endpaper. Modern pressure-sensitive tape uses an acrylic adhesive which can be removed with heat or commercial solvents. Older cellophane tapes used adhesives that would oxidize over time, becoming brittle and leaving a stain. These adhesives rarely respond to anything but heat and gentle coaxing with a blunt tool. The staining transference may not removable.

Solution A:

1. Apply a small gel-type heating pad to the item.
2. Coax edge of the label or tape up with paring knife or micro spatula.

Solution B:

1. Using an iron, apply low heat until the item begins to peel. If needed, cover surface with a sheet of white paper to protect from overheating.
2. Coax edge of label or tape up with paring knife or micro spatula.
3. Continue to apply heat from the edges toward the middle until offending item is removed.

Solution C:

1. Apply heat using a quilting iron, heat transfer tool or precision temperature tool from various vendors. Even a soldering iron with a spade tip or applied to the tip of a spatula.
2. Coax edge of label or tape up with a paring knife, spatula, or plastic scraper.

Solution D:

1. Using a cotton swab, apply lighter fluid/naphtha to the edge of the offending item.

2. As the naphtha dissolves the adhesive, coax the edge of the label up with a paring knife, spatula, or plastic scraper.

3. Continue to apply naphtha underneath the edges, peeling up as you go.

4. When removed, wash residue off area with more naphtha.

Caution: Do not combine heat and solvent methods at the same time.

Note: bookseller trade labels are about 1" in size and were pasted into new books along the bottom edge of the inside front or back cover. They were fairly common from about the 1860's to the 1970's and a terrific memento mori of the bookselling trade. Many famous yet deceased bookstores live on only with these tiny reminders. These evidences of provenance usually complement the book and enhance the sale, and do not need to be removed.

LIBRARY POCKETS

Problem: Circulating ex-library books will almost always have book pockets, except when a library sale volunteer has torn out the entire page. Pockets were applied with rubber cement until the mid 1970's, when peel and stick pockets were introduced. Both types should respond well to the application of heat and other sticker removing methods, except where the rubber cement has oxidized and there is not much moisture to allow the cement to soften.

Solution A:

1. Remove as much of the pocket as possible without prying up the adhered sections. This will involve a knife or razor blade.

2. Treat remaining sections like stickers or tape. Apply a warm quilting or clothes iron and gently pry up with spatula or plastic scraper.

Solution B:

1. Using a cotton swab or small paint brush, apply sticker solvent under the edges

2. Gently work the pocket remains up with a spatula or plastic scraper.

BOOKPLATES

Problem: A bookplate has been pasted onto an endpaper. Library pastes are water activated and can be removed with the application of more water. In the last two decades "sticker" book plates have become popular. You can usually assume that a glossy bookplate is a sticker and refer to the sticker removal section. The following solution is for non-glossy bookplates.

Solution A:

1. Cut a piece of paper towel to the size of the plate with 1" overlap.

2. Soak the paper towel in sterile or filtered water, squeeze until just damp inside another paper towel.

3. Place the damp paper towel over the book plate. If the plate is on the free endpaper, place watercolor or blotter paper under the endpaper and then a sheet of wax paper or plastic between the endpaper and the following page.

4. Cover the paper towel with wax paper or plastic and close the book; leave under weight 30 minutes to 1 hour.

5. Check to see if the paste has begun to release. Carefully pry up the plate with a blunt knife or micro spatula.

6. Wipe the area with crumpled damp paper towels to remove any residual paste.

7. Once the bookplate has been removed, cover page with dry watercolor or blotter paper and put under weight for several hours or iron dry with clothes iron.

Note: If a bookplate is from a previous non-library owner, particularly if it is decorative, it is part of the provenance of the book and may add to its appeal.

Solution B:

1. Brush surface and edges of book plate with Stamp Lift® fluid.

2. As the adhesive begins to release from the paste down, slowly peel up the book plate.

3. Use more Stamp Lift fluid if plate is stubborn.

4. When the book plate is removed, go over the area with Stamp Lift and a cotton ball or clean towel.

WRITING

Problem: Someone who is not noteworthy and NOT the author has decorated the book with signatures, annotations, marginalia, or library indexing.

Solution A: Use a series of erasers, starting with soft white vinyl eraser and graduating, if needed, to grittier gray ink eraser.

Solution B: Use an electric eraser with a white vinyl cartridge and graduate to grittier red rubber or gray ink cartridges.

Solution C: In some cases, ultra fine sandpaper or a sanding sponge can be applied with care, so as not to wear a hole in the paper.

Covers. Forever isn't just for diamonds. Indelible ink applied to book cloth or leather or non-glossy covered books is permanent. Some permanent marker can be removed from glossy paper-back surfaces with M.E.K. (methyl ethyl ketone) or acetone (nail polish remover); however anything strong enough to remove the ink can eat through the gloss and attack the print on the book cover. Light applications with cotton balls are advised.

Paper. If the writing is on an endpaper and is still bright and unfaded, it was most likely written in Sharpie® marker or other indelible ink. Permanent markers are made with solvents and dyes, instead of pigments. Pigment-based markers, such as highlighters, will fade over time.

Any chemical that can reliquify the dyes will only make a bigger mess. Chlorine bleach will only lighten the color; in the case of black it will turn it yellow, and red will go to pink. It will also damage the paper and boards, as some components in bleach never evaporate and will continue to break down the fibers over time.

The only way to remove the marker is to remove the offending endpapers. If you can't find or buy an endpaper to match, you can use the rear free endpaper; it is an easier flaw to accept if this endpaper is missing (rather than the front free endpaper). If the marker is on the pastedown, use a free endpaper to replace it and replace the rear free endpaper with one that is a close match.

Note: It is generally more work than it is worth to replace an endpaper due to a simple owner's signature or library stamp. Most people are not bothered by previous owner signatures or even consider that they add to the provenance of the book.

Problem: A budding artist has personalized a copy of a favorite book. It is almost impossible to remove crayon completely without a lot of money and motivation. Crayon dyes leach into the paper fibers beneath, but some accidental artworks can be made less severe.

Solution A:

1. Carefully use a paring knife or spatula to scrape off as much crayon as possible.

2. Cover the inscription with blotter or watercolor paper and apply a clothes iron to the area; this will cause some crayon to melt and adhere to the blotter paper.

3. Use a white vinyl eraser on the remaining marks, graduate to an ink eraser.

4. Repeat until you get tired or give up!

Solution B:

1. Spread rubber cement thickly on the crayon, when dry, roll off rubber cement.

2. Use a white vinyl eraser on the remaining mark, graduate to an ink eraser.

3. Repeat until you get tired or give up!

CALL NUMBERS

Problem: Old library call written numbers are inscribed on the book spine. These were written in either a paint-like ink or inscribed with a hot stylus and usually coated with clear lacquer to prevent them from chipping off.

Solution:

1. Color test lacquer-removing solvents against the buckram. Usually, the turn inside the hollow back is a good place to color test.

2. If the color test is satisfactory, apply solvent to the area with a cotton cosmetic round or swatch of cotton rag.

3. Remove the layer of clear lacquer from around the call numbers and discard rag.

4. Begin again on the letters with the solvent on the cloth. Try to dab UP the white lacquer as it liquefies, do not smear it against the buckram.

5. When you have removed as much as you can, wash the area with another course of solvent and clean rags.

These solvents can be successful for removing call numbers:

- Nail polish remover (acetone)
- 91% isopropyl alcohol
- toluene
- Ditzler Lacquer Thinner®

Caution. Take care not to use a solvent that removes the color from the book cloth as well. You may end up with a lightened spot where the call letters used to be, and then have to use something like Meltonian Shoe Creme or leather dye to even off the color. But, depending on the value of the book, this may be preferable to glaring white call letters.

Correction Fluid

Problem: Someone has painted white correcting fluid over their name on the front endpaper. There are many types of correction fluid available: White Out® Quick Dry, White Out® Extra Coverage, White Out® Water Based, and Liquid Paper®, all with slightly different formulations.

Solution: The best removal results come from odorless mineral spirits (white spirits), naphtha, heptane, and turpentine. All successfully liquefy the correction fluid, which then must be removed quickly. Heptane also makes Liquid Paper congeal, and so gives the cleanest result. White Out Water Based® will not re-liquefy with anything except paint stripper.

1. Apply solvent to the affected area with a cosmetic round or swatch of cotton rag.

2. Work on small sections at a time, drawing the correction fluid away from the surface.

3. Discard the work rag frequently, as these solvents evaporate as fast as you use them. And partially liquefied correction fluid may smear.

NOTE: Mineral spirits, naphtha, and turpentine are all found in the paint section of your hardware store. Mineral spirits, naphtha and heptane all work well to remove stickers cleanly and quickly. Heptane can most easily be found at art supply stores, sold as Bestine® Rubber Cement Thinner and Solvent.

LEAVES

LOOSE LEAF

Problem: The text block is tight but one leaf is detached from the book. This can be the result of many things; with perfect bound books, it can be one or a cluster of pages that just detach the first time the book is read.

Solution A: a single detached leaf

1. Open the book to the place where the leaf ought to be.

2. Lay the leaf against the edge of the table and using a small paint brush, brush a minute amount of PVA against the gutter edge. Be careful not to over-glue the top and bottom corners.

3. Insert the leaf into its place in the gutter, lining it up with the other pages.

4. Close the book and leave it under weight overnight.

Solution B: three or more detached leaves in one spot

1. Group the leaves tightly together with the spine edges lined up evenly. Secure with spring clips along the top and bottom if need be.

2. Lay the grouping against the edge of the table and using a small paint brush, brush a minute amount of PVA against the "spine" edge of this bundle.

3. Allow to dry, then add another layer of adhesive to the "spine" of the bundle.

4. Insert the bundle into its place in the gutter, lining it up with the other pages.

5. Close the book and leave it under weight overnight.

Torn Leaf

Problem: A leaf is still attached but has an open or closed tear. The solution depends on the severity of the tear. A "closed tear" is one where the edges still match up. An "open tear" is one where some paper is missing along the edges of the tear.

Solution A: (Use for a very small closed tear)

1. Slide a piece of baking parchment under the torn leaf.

2. Apply a thin layer of methyl cellulose over the tear.

3. Place another piece of baking parchment over the tear and iron dry.

Solution B: (Use for a larger closed tear)

1. Cut a piece of archival repair tape to closely match the tear.

2. Removing backing and carefully apply to the tear.

3. Rub the tape firmly with a bone folder. The heat from the friction activates the adhesive and will make the tape less visible.

NOTE: While this repair is permanent, the tape may be removed with mineral spirits if desired. Two widths – 1/2" and 1" – are available from most vendors.

Solution C: (Use for an open tear)

1. Slide a piece of blotter or watercolor paper under the torn leaf.

2. Tear off a 1/2" strip of Japanese mending tissue to match the length of the tear plus 1/4." The width should overlap the tear by 1/8" inch. Feather the edges of the mending tissue by lightly wetting it and coaxing the fibers apart.

3. Apply thinned paste or methyl cellulose to a piece of wax paper or poly.

4. Apply the tissue to the paste and gently lift up with paring knife. There should be an even layer of paste on the tissue.

5. Apply the tissue to the tear.

6. Cover with wax paper or poly.

7. Close book and leave under weight overnight.

8. Remove blotter paper and peel off poly.

Folded Leaf

Problem: Someone has dog eared a page or a page has an accidental fold in it.

Solution A:

1. Slide a piece of firm card stock under the bent page.

2. Cover the page with a piece of copy paper. The starchy paper will protect the page from overheating or any transfer from the iron surface.

3. Apply a medium clothes or quilting iron over the spot.

Solution B:

1. Slide a piece of firm card stock under the bent page.

2. Use distilled water and a soft paint brush or cotton swab, almost dry, to dab minute amount of water along the fold. This will cause the paper fibers to swell.

3. Cover the page with a piece of copy paper. The starchy paper will protect the page from overheating or any transfer from the iron surface.

4. Apply a medium clothes or quilting iron over the spot.

Loose Signature

Problem: All the signatures line up except for one, which is sticking out from the rest. It is not fully detached, just out of sync.

Solution:

1. Lay the book on its side and open to the offending signature.

2. Run a piece of string through the center fold of the loose signature so that the ends hang out.

3. Turn back to the first page of the signature and run a very thin thread of glue in the gutter of the book behind the signature.

4. Close the book and gently tug both ends of the string toward the spine until the signature is in line with the rest.

5. Put the book under weight overnight.

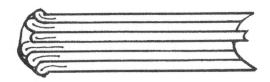

Embossed Page

Problem: An embosser has imprinted a circular mark, usually on the title page. This is almost impossible to remove COMPLETELY, however it can be made less severe. This can take a long time and in the end the mark will still be visible, but it can be a nice touch to improve personal or shelf copies.

Solution:

1. Place blotter or watercolor paper under the embossed page.

2. Lightly apply distilled or filtered water with a Q-tip® or small paint brush to a small part of the embossing. Keep at it until the paper fibers swell.

3. Iron the swollen fibers flat with an iron.

4. Repeat the process over the same spot and continue through the entire mark.

MISSING/DAMAGED ENDPAPERS

Replacing an endpaper or even all the endpapers is not a crime. Endpapers have always been replaceable. The endpaper is the final piece the binder applies to cover up all the unattractive parts of the fine work he or she has just done. It also tightens the bond between the text block and the binding and prevents the boards from warping.

Saving endpapers from damaged and discarded books is a helpful trick of many booksellers. Blank and nearly blank pages from textbooks and other reference books can be used. Even if a page has two or three lines on it, the page can be cut down to fit a smaller book. (You can experiment with bleaching the ink off a page, but you will never be happy with the result. By the time you remove the ink you will also be removing any patina and foxing the paper has in it and it will never really match.)

NOTE: Keep loose endpapers in a file drawer sorted into folders by height; you can put colored, patterned and clay pages in other folders by hue. Use a light source such as a window to match the paper's age, watermarks and fiber content to a page from the book itself.

Clay coated endpapers. Artex makes clay paper similar to the kind found in late 19thc publishers' bindings. It is difficult to work with as every scratch shows up, but if you really need it there is no substitute. The backing paper is snow white, so you need to paste a vintage paper over it for the front endpaper, which then makes it noticeably thick, so I don't advise using it unless you are a masochist.

MISSING FREE ENDPAPER

Problem: The front or rear free endpaper is damaged or missing.

Solution A:

1. Replace with another vintage end paper. In an extreme case, you can buy a cheap book with the proper vintage endpaper (such as a later printing) and then remove it and replace the missing one in the better book.

2. Cut to fit and tip it in as if it were a loose leaf.

Solution B:

1. Use the rear endpaper if no matching replacement is available. Its absence or replacement with a non-matching leaf is less noticeable.

2. Using a straight edge, gently tear out the rear endpaper and tip it in to replace the front endpaper.

DAMAGED PASTEDOWN

Problem: The front or rear pastedown endpaper is damaged.

Solution: If the pastedown has heavy ink or there are portions missing roughly exposing the board below, the endpaper must be removed before laying down a new one. Anything other than a smooth clean surface will be noticeable through the new endpaper. This procedure removes the entire endpaper – both the pastedown and the free endpaper – which are actually one sheet of paper in an undamaged book.

Remove endpaper:

1. Remove the free portion of the endpaper and gently peel off as much of the old pastedown endpaper as possible.

2. Place a damp paper towel over the remaining paper.

3. When the pasted paper becomes loose, gently remove it with a blunt paring knife or micro spatula

4. If the board beneath is still rough, it can be sanded with very fine sandpaper or a section of thin new paper can be pasted between the book cloth turns over the exposed portion.

Replace endpaper:

1. Measure the height of the old endpaper in three places, as it may not have been square to begin with: the outer edge of the pastedown, the inner hinge and the fore-edge of the free end-paper.

2. Measure the width using a string, from the outer edge of the turn-in on the inside cover, across the hinge, to the fore-edge of the text block.

3. Cut the endpaper to the exact height of the old one, cut the width with a +2 inch overhang.

4. Check the paper against the boards, and make a pencil tick where the hinge will be. Do not fold at this time.

5. Using a large soft brush, apply wheat paste to the pastedown section of the endpaper. Take care not to have too much excess paste in the hinge.

6. Carefully align the pasted corners with the previous endpa-pers, using a bone folder to smooth out the bubbles from the center outwards, and removing excess paste with clean paper towels.

7. Using a clean bone folder, lightly bone the endpaper into the hinge, but do not paste it. Insert wax paper or plastic between the endpaper and the text block. Close the book. With prac-tice, it is possible to paste the paper into the hinge at this

time. However, it can be done in two simple steps until you are good at it.

8. Let the paste-own dry overnight under a very heavy weight to prevent warping. A book or copy press would be ideal for this.

9. Open the book to the endpaper, remove any excess paste with clean paper towels.

10. Using a small clean brush, apply paste to the inside of the paper that will line the hinge. Smooth down with a bone folder, cover with wax paper or plastic, and set weights on top of the paper just along the hinge. Let dry.

11. When dry, run bone folder along the hinge and close the book.

12. Flip book over and lay flat on a table, so that the new endpaper is protruding from the fore-edge of the book along the table.

13. Insert a metal straight edge between the new endpapers and slide it to the edge of the text block. Cut free endpaper even with the text block.

14. You may want to repeat for the other end of the book, so that all of the endpapers match.

Spines

Cocked Spine

Problem: The book has a lean, tilt, or the spine is otherwise cocked to one side. This can be caused by excessive reading or mis-shelving, especially if the book was in a stack of leaning books.

Solution A: Lay the book on a flat surface and flip through its pages from back to front, smoothing the gutter as you go.

Solution B: Re-square the book by hand, wrap it in a roll-type bandage and put under weight for a few days or weeks.

Solution C: Steam book over a hot kettle for a few minutes then re-square book and put under weight for a few days.

Solution D: Put book in microwave for less than 10 seconds, re-square book and put under weight for a few days.

Shaken Hinge

Problem: The book in your hand feels like it has been read a hundred times. The text block is sagging away from the case. The hinges are not torn but they don't have a tight feel to them.

Solution:

1. Stand the book upright and spread the boards, opening the hollowback as wide as possible.

2. Coat a long thin stick (a dowel or thin knitting needle works well) with glue, NOT a lot of glue, just a smidgen.

3. Insert the stick into the hollowback and run it against the inside of the hinge on each side of the spine. Apply glue to the hinges, NOT the spine itself. If you are not adept at applying minute amounts of glue, roll a piece of wax paper into a tube and tuck it into the hollowback before you begin.

4. Close the book evenly and put it under weight overnight. It should sound crisp the first time you open it.

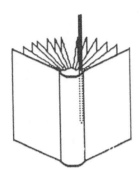

Weak Hinge

Problem: Book has a large text block that has been bound into a case using only the endpapers and no other reinforcement. With moderate to heavy use, the book will spend the rest of its days sagging in its case from its own weight. Normally, there should be a piece of cheesecloth-like substance called mull or super, that binds the text block to the case. The open weave has a large surface for glues to adhere, providing structural support.

Solution A: For a book that will have limited use, see the directions for shaken hinges.

Solution B: For a book that will get moderate to heavy use:

1. Cut a section of mull/super about twice the width of the spine and slightly longer than the book.

2. Insert this into the hollowback against the spine, making sure it covers the inside of both hinges where it will do the most good.

3. Insert the same length of wax paper or stiff plastic into the hollow as well; this strip should be wide enough to cover the inside of the backstrip and protect it from errant glue. To keep it out of the way, cut it very long, loop it around the back of the book and tape it to itself.

4. Coat a long thin stick with PVA, NOT a lot, just a smidgen.

5. Run a line of PVA inside the joint on both sides, making sure the fabric is IN the crease. You may want to do one side at a time. Remember you can always add more adhesive, but you cannot remove it.

6. Close the book and make sure the hinges are aligned correctly, perhaps using clean chopsticks or knitting needles to preserve the shoulder notch.

7. Leave under weight overnight.

8. The next day, open the book and check the hollowback and see if the joint is tight.

9. Remove the wax paper and trim the excess fabric from the top and bottom.

CRACKED HINGE

Problem: The endpaper covering the hinge is torn and the mull/super is visible but not torn. This can happen over time from excessive use or rough handling.

Solution:

1. Brace the front board on another book the same height so the endpaper is as evenly horizontal as possible.

2. Slowly work a mixture of methyl cellulose and PVA into the hinge with a paint brush or micro spatula. This will dry slower than straight PVA, allowing time to work the entire hinge.

3. As the frayed paper becomes moist, move it back into place over the hinge.

4. When finished, cover the hinge with wax paper and run your finger or bone folder gently down the hinge to smooth the repair and remove any bumps and air bubbles.

5. Insert wax paper aligned along the hinge, close the book, square it, put a stick in the shoulder and weight it overnight. The hinge dries tighter that way.

6. Allow the repair to dry in this position.

If the gap is still visible: When there is not enough endpaper to "fill in" the gap in the hinge, paste a 1/2" strip of medium weight Japanese paper over the repair.

1. Use a paint brush to wet a straight line a little over 1/2" away from the edge of the mending tissue.

2. Wet the straight edge of the tissue and feather the edge by pulling fibers away from the strip.

3. Place the Japanese paper strip on wax paper or plastic and apply wheat paste or methyl cellulose to it.

4. Pick up the paper with tweezers and apply it to the hinge like a bandage.

5. Cover the hinge with clean wax paper and smooth it down gently to remove bubbles and lumps.

6. Insert wax paper aligned along the hinge, close the book, square it, put a stick in the shoulder and weight it overnight.

7. Let dry overnight in this position.

CRACKED INTERNAL GUTTER

Problem: Two signatures in the book are just a little separated where the book has been cracked open, so there is a deep gutter, possibly with a peek at the mull or spine threads.

Usually this isn't a problem that needs fixing, but if it stands out it must be pretty obvious. Most often, the cracked gutter scenario occurs when you have heavy art books or illustrated plates come away from their facing pages or a book has been forced open too widely, for example, to be copied or scanned.

Solution: The fix is similar to tipping in a page without the page. The secret to gluing paper is that "less is more": the more you use, the more difficult you make it for yourself.

1. Apply the smallest amount of PVA to the edge of a clean index card or piece of card stock, by running the edge of the card through the edge of a small glue puddle. Ideally, there should be no rounded glue bubble on the card, just a smooth smear. If you pick up too much glue, you can wipe your index card against scrap paper to remove some. What you want to end up with is an index card with a thin shiny stripe down the edge.

2. Open the cracked section as widely as possible.

3. Slide the index card down the gutter against the facing page.

4. Lay a piece of wax paper in between the two pages but not all the way into the gutter. Don't try to push the wax paper all the way into the gutter.

5. Close the book, weight overnight, and in the morning tug the wax paper out.

MISSING HEADBAND

Problem: A cloth headband is missing. Many late 19th century publisher's bindings had strips of ticking fabric for headbands. Stitched headbands are more common before the industrial revolution and later on in fine bindings.

Solution A: Use ready made headband yardage available from bindery supply houses. Available in silk and cotton, and many colors, they may "look" replaced as they are too "nice" for some old publishers' bindings. (You can soak it in tea, coffee, or apply diluted leather dye and dry to age it a bit.) Cut headband to fit, test fit, apply PVA along lower half, insert and press against top of spine.

Solution B:

1. Cut a 2" x 3" swatch of finely striped cotton fabric. Striped ticking fabric can usually be found in basic blue, red, green, brown and black stripes, which are just right for 19th century use.

2. If you want that century-old dingy color (so headband doesn't look "new") soak the swatch first in tea, coffee or diluted leather dyes and let dry thoroughly.

3. Soak the swatch in laundry starch, wheat starch, or methyl cellulose.

4. Fold swatch in half over a piece of thin cotton twine. The string should be firmly in the crease. Rub down.

5. Squeeze out the excess moisture and let dry, on a piece of wax paper or plastic.

6. When dry, peel it up.

7. Soak in tea, coffee or diluted leather dyes to give it that century old dirty color.

8. Cut to fit, test fit, apply PVA to lower half, insert and press against top of spine.

MISSING RIBBON MARKER

Problem: One of more ribbon markers are missing from a book. This happens quite frequently with personal bibles and journals. The exposed part of the ribbon deteriorates faster than the hidden part.

Solution:

1. Cut 1/8" satin ribbon the length of the book, plus at least 2 more inches.

2. If more than one ribbon is missing, glue the ends of the ribbon to a ½" piece of card stock and let dry.

3. Open the book as wide as possible; ideally pulling the boards back towards the spine, until you can see down into the hollowback.

4. Dab PVA on end of the ribbon or of the piece of cardstock.

5. Using blunt tweezers or a micro spatula, tuck the ribbon into the spine and press against the binding near the top.

6. Tuck a piece of plastic or wax paper into the hollowback before the covers are released to ensure no glue transfers from inside of spine to the spine covering.

7. Let dry overnight, and remove the wax paper.

8. Trim the ribbon as desired.

SPLIT SPINE (PERFECT BOUND PAPERBACK)

Problem: The spine is broken into two or more pieces. This is a complicated repair and may not turn out well the first few times, so I strongly suggest you practice it first on some worthless paperbacks!

Solution:

1. Remove the entire case – front and back cover and spine covering. If the paper cover of the spine is also split, try to salvage as much of the spine covering as possible. Set aside.

2. Align the text block and using deep c-clamps (or a lying press) secure it between pieces of heavy cardboard or masonite at least as long as the spine and as tightly as possible. Line the boards up evenly about 1/8" under the shoulder of the spine. (Point the back of the c-clamps away from the book.)

3. **For spines larger than 1":** Using a backing saw, cut three or four 1/16th inch deep grooves across the back of the spine. Take a strand from a piece of hemp twine and coat it with glue, lay it in the groove, pull it tightly, and tape the ends of the twine to the board. (The twine should not protrude from the spine, i.e., your grooves should be deep enough to allow the twine to lay flush with the spine surface.) Allow to dry overnight. Trim the ends of the twine flush with the edge of the spine.

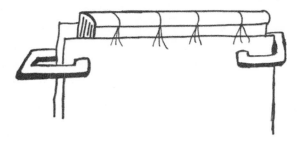

4. **For all spines:** Coat the spine with thick glue and lay a piece of mull or super across the entire spine; brush with more glue to ensure that the glue fills in the mesh. Let dry overnight. If necessary, add a third c-clamp in the center to give added pressure while drying.

5. Take the reassembled book out from between the boards and c-clamps.

6. Trim the mull flush with the top and bottom of the spine. If the book is wider than 1" you may want to allow about 1/16th to extend beyond the sides of the spine for added security.

7. **Reconstruct the cover:**

   a. If the front, back, and spine covering are all undamaged, you can use binders or archival tape on reverse side to reattach the pieces to each other. Take care to size the fit against the book, as the new spine is slightly wider than it was when it was new.

   b. If any of the pieces are incomplete, reassemble the cover on new card stock sized to fit over the old text block. Using thinned glue, attach the printed cover sections to the card stock. Taking care to glue all the way to the edges of the old cover. Let the new cover dry under weight overnight, protected by wax paper or plastic.

8. Refit the new cover to the book, making sharp folds at the shoulders. Using glue, attach the new cover to the spine. Wrap the book tightly with an Ace® or other roll-type bandage. Let dry overnight.

SEMI-DETACHED COVER

Problem: The cloth case of a hollowback book is intact, but one cover is partly or completely detached from the text block (both the end paper and the underlying mull is torn, but not the cloth cover itself). The cloth backstrip is thus partly or wholly loose from the book as well.

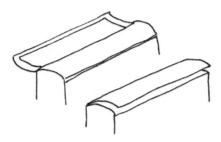

Solution: The hollowback is basically a tube formed between the case and the text block; a new tube form needs to be inserted, to which the spine cloth and the cover edge will adhere. Note: this is a complex repair – practice first on a worthless book.

Make a hollow paper tube.

1. Use a piece of bond weight paper (acid f if possible) if it has a grain make sure running parallel to the spine. (copier ; computer paper are grainless but may be a heavy enough weight)

2. Cut it about '1/4" shorter than the heigh the text block and three times the widtl the spine, less about 1/4".

3. Fold the paper in thirds along the short a like a letter folded to be placed in an er

lope (i.e., fold up the bottom third and then fold the top third down over it).

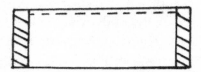

4. Lightly paste the edge of top flap to the second flap

5. Place the tube on the work surface with the two-layer side on top.

6. Using a straight-edge mark a line 1/2" down from the top from the top and 1/2" up from the bottom.

7. Cutting through just the top 2 layers of the tube, remove the notch at the top and bottom of the spine. This will leave one side of the tube the full length of the book while the other side is 1/2" shorter at the top and bottom.

Apply the tube to the spine of the book.

1. Using a brush, lightly apply a diluted PVA, wheat paste or a mixture of PVA and methyl cellulose to one long side of the paper tube.

2. Center the tube to the spine of the book.

3. Quickly check that the backstrip and cover fit exactly back into place without any bumps, and that the detached cover lines up exactly with the edge of the text block. If it does not, peel up the tube and realign or make a new tube the correct size.

4. Rub the entire tube firmly with the flat of the bone folder; smoothing out all bubbles, the friction will help spread the adhesive and speed the drying.

5. Use the brush to apply more adhesive to the rest of the tube, including the shoulders; taking care not to get adhesive inside the tube.

6. Wrap the backstrip and cover back over the tube.

7. Use a clean bone folder to smooth the backstrip into place and work the book cloth around the shoulder and into the joint.

8. Cover the spine with wax paper or a comic book bag.

9. Wrap the book tightly in a rolled bandage and let dry overnight.

10. The next day, check the fit on the previously broken hinge. Use a small paint brush of adhesive to make sure the hinge is secure. If there is still a gap along the hinge, follow the steps for a cracked hinge repair.

BOARDS

BUMPED CORNER

Problem: The corners of the boards have been bumped to the point where they have curved inward and are possibly smashed and feathery.

Solution A:

1. If the bumping is limited to fraying and a slight curl, rub some wheat paste into the corner.

2. Protect corner with wax paper or plastic

3. Sandwich the corner between small pieces of cardboard

4. Secure with bulldog clip or small c-clamp.

5. Leave overnight to dry.

Solution B:

1. Using a very small brush or a piece of cardboard, insert minute amounts of diluted PVA or methyl cellulose between the feathered layers of the cardboard corner. Do not glue the cloth to the cardboard at this time.

2. Firmly press the layers together and remove any excess adhesive.

3. Protect corner with wax paper or plastic.

4. Sandwich the corner between small pieces of cardboard.

5. Secure with bulldog clip or small c-clamp.

6. Leave overnight to dry.

7. Remove clamp, cardboard, and wax paper.

8. Use paste or methyl cellulose to reattach the book cloth to the corner. Gently tug it around the edges to fit.

9. Replace wax paper, cardboard, and clamps.

10. Remove reinforcements when dry.

Bubbled Cloth

Problem: The book's cover has been wet. Bubbles and wrinkles have formed in the book cloth as it dried, and it is no longer uniformly tight against the board.

Solution:

1. Apply a thin coat of methyl cellulose to the area, making sure it soaks through the cloth. (If the bubble isn't very big, you can get away with just using a bit of distilled or filtered water on a clean rag, but test the colorfastness of the book cloth before applying it.)

2. If the board is not embossed, you can iron it dry through blotter paper. Otherwise cover with plastic, wax paper, or parchment and let dry under weight overnight.

3. When the entire surface has dried completely, remove the excess paste with a damp cloth.

Discolored Cloth or Leather

Problem: The color of the book cloth or leather is no longer even. This can be caused by water or sun. Fabrics used for bookbinding are not meant to be washed with water; the dyes aren't colorfast and easily bleed. Leather bindings stored in sunlight fade easily but can be redyed a darker color.

For dark-colored cloth or leather

Solution A:

1. Wrap the text block in plastic or wax paper.

2. Dye the exterior surface with a diluted alcohol-based leather dye of a darker color, using a clean rag or cotton balls.

3. Use cotton swabs on the edges, turns, and gutter. Be extremely careful on the turns, as the dye will be absorbed into the paper.

4. Remove excess dye from gilded lettering with cotton swabs and alcohol.

Solution B: A light application the nearest color of Meltonian Shoe Cream. Apply with cosmetic round or clean rag, let stand for an hour or so then remove the excess.

For light-colored cloth

Solution A: Wash the entire cloth cover with 50/50 water and all purpose cleaner applied with a clean cotton rag. This may more evenly distribute the color. Do not let the water soak into the cover.

Solution B: An application of Clean Cover Gel can also distribute color more evenly.

Wet Book

Problem: The book is freshly wet, not for more than a day or so, after that the book may be irrecoverable and when it dries it will carry the scars.

Solution:

1. Blot as much water from the book as possible. Put blotter paper or paper towels between the pages and place under weight or in a book press.

2. Stand the book on its tail and fan open the pages. Dry the book in this position in sunlight or with a fan away from a direct heat source, but in a warm dry area. The more quickly the book dries, the less page rippling will occur.

3. If the cover is still warped, place the book between two press boards and place under weight or in a book press for several days.

4. Usually a wet book that has been air dried will never look great again.

Warped Boards

Problem: The covers of the book are warped and one or both no longer lies flat against the text block. This can happen when a book is mis-shelved and uneven pressure has caused the book to bend for a prolonged time.

Solution:

1. Put a damp paper towel or piece of blotter or watercolor paper on the rear pastedown endpaper, cut to fit just inside the turns.

2. But a waterproof barrier between this and the text block (such as a sheet of plastic wrap or wax paper).

3. Close the book and do the same to the front pastedown.

4. Put the book in a book or copy press or under a lot of weight for a few days.

5. Check the book, you should have made a good start at coaxing the fibers back into shape.

6. Repeat the process as needed.

Hazards

Mold and Mildew

Problem: Live molds and mildews can kill you – or at least make you wish you were dead. Exposure to mold can lead to debilitating allergies even among people not prone to them. Toxigenic molds, like the common "black mold," produce mycotoxins which are toxic to the cells of higher plants and animals, including humans.

Mold and mildew are generic terms that refer to various types of fungi, which are microorganisms that depend on other organisms for sustenance. Mold propagates by disseminating large numbers of airborne spores, which travel to new desirable locations to germinate. Molds excrete enzymes that allow them to digest organic materials, such as paper and book bindings, altering and weakening those materials. In addition, they may contain colored substances that can stain paper, cloth, or leather. The only way to control their growth is to control humidity and temperature and prevent the addition of new active mold.

Visible Mold

Solution A:

1. Don't bring any books with live mold or mildew into your home!

Solution B:

1. Wrap book loosely in wax paper and put in freezer for 2-3 days. Freezing generally kills mold and mildew.

2. Stand book in the sun with pages fanned open for several days – sunlight also kills mold and mildew and reduce mold odor.

Solution C:

1. Wear a face mask and latex gloves.

2. Bracket the page with wax paper or plastic

3. Apply 95% pure alcohol with a soft cloth. Alcohol with a larger percentage of water content may stain the book or saturate the pages.

4. Leave book under weight overnight

Solution D: Throw the book away, particularly if you see black mold.

MOLD ODOR

Solution: Wipe the exterior with a cloth laced with disinfectant, such as Lysol®. Repeat if necessary and keep the item dry and segregated. Do not replace the item in the collection until you are certain the mold and mildew have not resurfaced.

UNPLEASANT ODORS

Problem: The book stinks – literally. Books and paper are highly absorbent and will pick up the odor of anywhere they have been stored. Storage areas that are conducive to even minor amounts of mold and mildew will impart that smell on books. As will areas with cigarette smoke, mothballs, wood stoves, cigars, pipes, perfumes, a coal cellar, and foodstuffs.

NOTE: For solutions A-E, the length of time will vary depending on the strength of the odor and the types of materials from which the book is made. Leave the book for at least two weeks and then check again every two weeks to see if the odor has improved. Some books may require a month or more.

Solution A: Put the book in a zippered plastic bag or airtight container with a plain charcoal briquette.

Solution B: Put the book in a brown paper bag with crumpled newspapers.

Solution C: Put the book in zippered plastic bag or airtight container with an unscented fabric softener sheet.

Solution D: Put the book in zippered plastic bag or airtight container with unscented cat litter.

Solution E: Put the book in zippered plastic bag or airtight container with Book Deodorizer®.

Solution F: Wipe the exterior of the book with a clean rag sprayed with a fabric refreshener or odor remover, especially the kind sold in pet stores. The active ingredient in Febreze® is cyclodextrin, a modified starch which will not harm the average book.

ACIDIC MATERIALS

Problem: Printed items, such as dust jackets or manuscript pages, are in danger of deteriorating from the acid content they contain. Usually at-home deacification is limited to paper items, newspaper, and dust jackets.

Books made before the industrial age, i.e., with paper from cloth fibers and covered in leather, are more chemically stable than books made after the mid-19th century. The mass production of the industrial age brought in materials with more wood pulp and a higher acid content. Papers produced well into the 20th century were made with an alum rosin, which is acidic. Acidic paper loses its strength, becomes brittle, and is unable to support itself.

In a perfect world, all books would be made of alkaline paper, which lasts ten times longer than customary acidic paper, which crumbles after about 40 years. Permanent papers, such as those sized with a buffering agent like calcium carbonate have a life expectancy of 500 years or more.

More or less pH is a measure of the acidity or alkalinity of a solution. Less than seven is considered acidic and greater than seven is considered alkaline; a pH of 7.0 is considered neutral. Materials with a pH of 7.0 or higher are considered acid-free. Acid-free materials can be either buffered or unbuffered. Buffering agents like magnesium oxide or calcium carbonate typically raise the pH of a material to 8.0 or higher. A good rule of thumb is to assume all paper items are acidic unless clearly labeled or you have tested it.

TESTING

pH Testing pen. pH testing can be done with a pen that is similar to the ones used to test money. Lineco markets a pH testing pen that can distinguish between safe (neutral or alkaline) paper and board and acidic materials. Simply draw a small line on the material you wish to test. The chlorophenol red indicator solution in the pen will turn purple on any paper with a pH of 6.8 and above. A clear or yellow color indicates the material is probably unsuitable for conservation purposes. Paper can be respectably long lived if is pH is as low as 6.0, especially if is well made and carefully used and stored. In order to last for centuries in today's polluted air, it must have an alkaline reserve and this usually means a pH of 7.0 or greater. Unfortunately the mark from this pen does not fade entirely. If anyone knows of one that DOES fade, please let me know.

Litmus paper. Before you use a water-based product you are unfamiliar with for cleaning or repair, you may want to check its pH balance. Litmus strips can be found very cheap online; on eBay for example 100 strips sell for about $4. If an item is NOT water based or is a solid such as a piece of paper, you will need to soak or mix it with water and then test the water (assuming the water is pH neutral).

DEACIDIFICATION

Solution: There are several deacidification sprays on the market for consumer use. The aerosol carrier evaporates quickly, leaving behind a layer of the buffering agent, which reacts with the moisture in the atmosphere to create the deacidificant. It would probably be best to scan or photograph the item before spraying, as there is a powdery residue.

1. Cover your work area with newsprint or a drop cloth.

2. Center the object to be deacidified.

3. Lightly spray the item from a distance of about 8-10 inches or whatever the manufacturer recommends.

4. Turn item over and repeat.

- Bookkeeper® Deacidification Spray (magnesium oxide)

- Papersaver® from Provenance, Inc. (calcium carbonate)

- Krylon Make it Acid-Free® Spray (calcium carbonate)

For further reading, see: The American Institute for Conservation - Observations on the Use of Bookkeeper® Deacidification Spray for the Treatment of Individual Objects (http://aic.stanford.edu/sg/bpg/annual/v15/bp15-17.html)

INSECTS

Problem: There is evidence of someone living in the book.

- **Silverfish** are carrot shaped, silvery, and have what look like antennae on both ends. They eat the starch used to size coated papers, the paste used to bind the book, and the ink off the page.

- **Firebrats** look almost exactly like silverfish, except for their mottled color.

- **Cockroaches** have a large, flat, oval body; hairy legs; and very long, slender antennae. They leave brown stains on paper and will eat almost anything.

- **Booklice** superficially resemble the lice of birds; they are soft-bodied, tiny insects that feed on the microscopic mold which grows on library materials in damp situations. They are fond of starch, starchy pastes, and the glue in books and wallpaper.

- **Crickets** will eat almost anything: plastic, wood, paper, leather, and fabric.

- **Termites** look like small white ants and eat the cover and pages in long, wiggly tracks.

Solution A: Don't buy books with bugs in them.

Solution B: Put the book in a zippered plastic bag in freezer below 20°F(-3°C) for several days.

Solution C: Put the book in a sealed container with a paper towel sprayed with an insecticide containing pyrethrins, a flea collar, or an insect strip for several days.

Solution D: Put the book in a zippered plastic bag in the microwave for 10 seconds.

Solution E: Put the book in a sealed container with a cake of dry ice for several days.

Solution F: Spray the book with insecticide containing pyrethrins.

Solution G: Throw the book away.

Natural repellents: Many herbs repel one insect or another. A few of the following herbs, dried and crushed, will deter insects when sprinkled around the bookcase. Vacuum them up a few times a year and replace with a new batch. Or make sachets you can place on and around the bookcases.

- Balsam of Gilead
- Catnip
- Dried marigold
- Lavender
- Lemon eucalyptus
- Osage orange
- Pyrethrum (chrysanthemum flowers)
- Rosemary
- Sage
- Whole cloves
- Wormwood

PROTECTION

DUST JACKET COVER

Problem: The dust jacket is fragile, torn or just old and needs some added protection.

The dust jacket protector performs many functions: it guards against transference of dirt from hands, it provides a buffer between books on the same shelf (especially during transport), it protects books from the atmosphere in the room, it keeps small tears from becoming large tears and large tears from becoming fully detached pieces. It also keeps completely detached sections together in lieu of repair and it looks classy. You can get more for your book IN a dust jacket protector than out of one. A dust jacket protector ensures that a book will remain in the same condition as when it was cataloged.

Solution: There are many different styles and brands of dust jacket covers on the market. They all perform perfectly well. The few differences are in thickness and ease of use. Thinner covers (2mm) are useful for shelf copies and copies that don't get handled that much. Thicker covers are a must for heavy use and travel; libraries will use as much as a 4mm thick cover, whereas a bookseller who does many shows can use 3mm. When the jacket cover becomes scratched and dull, it should be replaced, as it doesn't make the book look any better regardless of how well it protects.

NOTE Dust jacket cover material comes in rolls as well as sheets. If you deal exclusively in one size, such as octavo modern firsts, you can save money by purchasing in bulk. There are also assorted sized packages, for the few times a larger cover is needed. Dust jacket covers are sold with and without liners. Books with brand new dust jackets can be wrapper with unlined covers; these have creased edges to hold the dust jacket safely. Damaged, fragile or old dust jackets need the stability of a dust jacket liner. Using dust jacket covers with liners that are open at the bottom allows you to fold and crease the dust jacket cover and liner to fit each book individually. Some, such as Brodart's Just-a-Fold® are pre-creased and perforated for a better fit.

When fitted properly, dust jacket covers should have no folds, no creases, no slack, and not extend further than a ½" beyond the edge of the dust jacket flap.

Fitting a Dust Jacket Cover

1. Roll out or lay out the dust jacket cover. When using rolled covers, use the dust jacket to gauge the length.

2. Slide the dust jacket into the cover, taking care to fit it snugly between the fold where the liner attaches to the film (if the cover is lined). Sometimes the jacket must be "wiggled" into place.

3. If the cover is not the exact size, fold up the bottom until the film is snug with the bottom edge of the dust jacket. Thumb crease the film in place, making certain that it is even the entire width of the dust jacket. One method is to tug UP towards the back of the table with the free hand while creasing with the thumb of the other.

4. Using a bone folder, sharply crease the folded film over the dust jacket. Begin in the center and crease out toward the sides of the dust jacket.

5. Wrap the dust jacket in its cover around the book, with the flaps protruding.

6. With the book fore-edge facing up, tuck the flaps in and thumb crease.

7. Remove the book and recrease the dust jacket in its cover using the bone folder

8. If the book is brand new, you can skip fitting the book into the jacket and simply crease the dust jacket folds after inserting into the cover. However, the dust jackets on many older books

have imprecise or over folded dust jacket flaps, requiring the book to be fitted first.

CLEAR BOOK COVER

Problem: An older book without a dust jacket needs protection.

Solution. Rolls of polyester film in varying thickness are available. These can be made into clear book jackets for protection: thin material (2mm) for shelf copies, and thicker material (3-4mm) for copies that will be handled and repeatedly transported. When these become dull and scratched, they should be removed and replaced, even if they are merely for protection.

1. Roll out the film on a cutting mat.

2. Place the book right side upon the film abutting the bottom edge.

3. Use a sharp knife to "mark" the film where the top of the book ends. It is no use to measure before cutting, as old books are notoriously inexact in size and even copies can differ in size from each other. Each cover needs to be unique.

4. Allowing for a "flap" two-thirds the width of the rear board, flip the book over right to left, so the rear cover is facing up.

5. Allow for a front flat of the same size and mark the end of the book cover.

6. Remove the book and set aside. NEVER use the book as a cutting edge.

7. Using a straight edge and the lines on the cutting mat, or a large t-square, cut the book jacket from the roll of film.

8. Remove the excess film from the cutting mat.

9. Replace the book in its original spot on the book cover, with the cover facing up and only the "flap" for the rear cover protruding from beneath the book.

10. Using the point of a bone folder, and the book as your straight edge, run a crease down the "fold" of the rear cover.

11. Put the book aside and fold the film on that crease, to make your rear flap. Use a bone folder to make that crease sharp. If the film is thick, you may need to do this twice and make a BOX shaped fold, enabling the film to lie flush against the book cover edge.

12. Put the rear cover of the book under the new flap and wrap the new book cover around the book.

13. Flip the book over from right to left so now the rear cover faces up and the front cover is against the cutting mat with the front "flap" protruding against the surface.

14. Use the bone folder to crease the fold, again.

15. Flip the book over left to right and use the bone folder to sharpen the crease of the fold.

16. Wrap the book in its new book cover; it should fit snugly without any slippage. Slippage may not seem like much now, but when shelved it could catch and damage fragile materials.

17. You may need the bone folder to make light creases where the book cover wraps around the spine; this will help the cover hug the book.

TEXT BLOCK WRAP

Problem: When working with liquids around books, such as oily dressings or dyes, it is best to wrap the text block and endpapers in thick butcher/brown paper or wax paper to protect them from harm.

Solution:

1. Use a piece of thick paper, 2½ to 3 times taller than the book.

2. Slide the paper into the rear gutter, between the rear cover and the text block.

3. Open the front cover.

4. Fold the top and bottom of the paper over the text block, and tape them down.

5. Fold down the paper surrounding the fore-edge, JUST like the corner of a gift package.

6. Secure fold with tape.

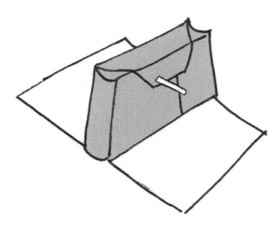

Ephemera

Booksellers often find themselves with various bits of ephemera. Old chipboard prints, postcards, greeting cards, baseball cards, or other carded ephemera may have many years of accumulated dirt and residue on them. Perhaps there is also tape residue on the corners, a few tears, and a bit of writing with pen and pencil.

Ephemera items such as these are generally constructed of layers, with printed paper outside and chipboard or cardboard at the center. If these get wet, the layers end up bubbling and separating. The card stock is not printed directly, but printed paper stock is adhered to the cardboard. The thicker the center layer, the less likely the cardboard is to curve or bend.

Staining. Dirt is either on the surface or in the case of stains it is beneath the surface. If it is beneath the surface, you will have to live with it. Some folks try "bleaching," but the bleach will alter the inks and will never stop breaking down the fibers; in 10 years the item will be dust.

Displaying. If delicate or damaged items are going to be framed, it is safer, easier, and more satisfying to have them scanned, clean the images digitally, and then frame new prints.

Surface Cleaning

Solution A: Start with small areas and gently go over the entire surface with a soft white vinyl eraser; anything harsher that soft white vinyl may injure old inks.

Solution B: Use a document cleaning bag, and sprinkling minute particles over one area at a time, gently rub these grains over the surface, follow up by blowing or lightly brushing the residue away with a soft brush.

Solution C: Make your own document cleaning bag/eraser crumbs by finely shredding an art gum or white vinyl eraser with a cheese grater. Sprinkle the particles over one area at a time, gently rub these grains over the surface, follow up by blowing or lightly brushing the residue away with a soft brush.

Solution D: Use Absorene® and sprinkle the particles onto the surface, then lightly rub/roll the pieces back and forth over the dirty parts, applying just enough pressure to cause some friction. Blow or brush the particles off the surface. Repeat with clean particles.

Removing Residue

The older an adhesive is, the harder it is to remove. Modern tapes have an acrylic adhesive which responds both to heat and to heptane (Bestine Solvent or Undu) or lighter fluid/ naphtha. These highly evaporative chemicals will also not hurt the inks.

If you cannot get the residue off with lighter fluid and a Q-tip, try heat. Use a quilting iron, a clothes iron, or even a hair drier to warm it enough to roll it off. There are rubber "crepe" erasers used for removing rubber cement that work well for rolling soft adhesive.

Older cellophane tapes used a synthetic rubber compound which oxidizes over time and becomes hard. Though not reactive to chemicals, these tapes MAY still come off with heat. Professionals (people with more than average patience) use heat applied to small spatulas to slowly work the old tape off the surface.

The discoloration left from old tapes is a stain and not further residue. If the stain does not respond to the gentle abrasion of an ink eraser, it should be ignored.

Storing Ephemera

Problem: Non-book items don't shelve well. They are floppy and can become accidentally damaged. To keep their value and preserve their condition, like items should be stored in properly sized containers.

Newsprint. Unlike other papers, newsprint is made from the cheapest possible materials; when it is milled, the lignin is not removed from the pulp. It is the lignin that causes the paper to rapidly become brittle and yellow when exposed to air and/or sunlight. A newspaper is rapidly aging even while you are reading it.

Solution: Archival quality acid-free containers (boxes and bags) are available in an infinite variety of shapes and sizes from many vendors. University Products is one of the best catalogs for these materials. The drawback to storage in archival boxes is that items are not readily available to transport and show to potential customers.

After any needed deacidification or repair, paper ephemera should be stored in non-reactive clear plastic bags. Ultra Pro comic book bags also come in a seemingly infinite range of sizes, from baseball card sized to poster sized.

For transport or display, bagged paper items should be stored in art portfolios or acrylic top loaders. By keeping the item poly bagged, the item can be removed for examination without damage or staining.

Many dealers use 3" wide three-ring binders to display ephemeral material. These do not make a good long-term storage solution. They do not make a good display solution for that matter, as the bulk of the binder works against the items' safety. Unless the binder is only half filled and the plastic pages are turned precisely, they tend to curve and buckle and this curvature translates through to the ephemera. One to two inch binders or small portfolios work best for displaying soft storage pages, and an upright box makes a suitable "flip file" for items stored in firm protectors, such as acrylic top loaders.

Scan it. Ephemeral items should be scanned at a high resolution while being catalogued and before they are put into storage.

This will prevent overhandling and document the condition at the moment of acquisition. Delicate pages stored in plastic sleeves can be scanned while still in the plastic sleeves. A low-res image can made from the hi-res image for use in promotion. This will prevent any further deterioration of the material from light exposure and repeated scanning.

Deacidify it. Scan or photograph the item before you spray it with a buffering spray, as the buffering agents will leave a light coating of dust, which can be removed after the chemicals have had a chance to perform their magic,

Reinforce it. Because the item is already fragile and probably folded, it needs to be stored against a pH neutral backing board. All of the archival suppliers sell acid-free boards, the most commonly available are comic book backing boards. See Vendors: Bagsunlimited.com or University Products.

Protect it. If you need this item to be seen by potential buyers, you need to put it in some form of plastic. Polyethylene, polypropylene or polyester (Mylar) polybags come in an unbelievable range of sizes; up to and including poster size. Just make sure they have been OK'd for long term storage and you are burying from a reputable seller.

Hide it. Once you have the item secured to a backboard and encased in a polybag, don't leave it out in the light. Or anywhere a corner can get bent or dinged or just wrecked, because the item is too big. Make or buy an art portfolio. There are some ridiculously cheap ones designed for art students; 17" x 22" plastic/zippered cases for under $20. There is NO reason not to have something like this around to secure for objects for sale that are larger than 8"x 11". Personally I put things into it and shove it safely behind the desk, against the wall, where stuff won't get wrecked.

All of the above goes double and triple for holograph items, manuscripts and textiles. When in doubt, deacidify it; if it doesn't need it you won't hurt it. You want to support fragile items YET keep them available for examination.

SELF-ADHESIVE ALBUMS

Problem: Photographs are stuck in a self-adhesive "magnetic" photo album. After 10 or 20 years, these albums are reluctant to release the photographs from their sticky pages.

Solution:

1. Place a dish towel over the album page.

2. Lightly iron the page through the dish towel on low heat.

3. The photographs should pop off.

4. If the photos curl, the heat was too high. Let them cool on the counter under weigh for a while.

NOTE. This may also work if the images are attached with rubber cement, though it would be best to iron from the reverse side.

STORAGE

SHELVING

Obviously, book shelves should be straight and level as possible. For long-term storage, the back of the bookcase should be enclosed or flush against the wall. Aside from reducing the layers of dust, this will prevent too much moisture circulation and deter predators. Book shelves should not be varnished, or waxed, as the viscosity of these products can change depending on the ambient temperature.

Books should also be stored upright, and books that are close in size should be kept together to keep boards from warping. Books stored too loosely will lean to one side, causing cocked spines, and those stored too tightly together can cause warping, split joints, and torn headcaps.

Bookends are cheap and plentiful; the classic angled steel bookends work the best and cost the least. Decorative bookends may not weigh enough nor apply pressure evenly enough to do a proper job of propping up the books. Books themselves should not be used stacked as bookends permanently. A stack of books can list to one side or the other, causing warping in the boards.

Oversized books should not be stored upright unless the entire shelf is of the same size. This will secure them from falling over when one or more is removed. Oversized books can be stored horizontally if there is no side pressure to cause board warping. It is also not a good idea to pile excess weight on them in this position.

Thick books such as unabridged dictionaries and lectern bibles should not be stored upright. These should be stored on their sides as they were meant to be. This can also be said for many case bound and hollowback books wider than 3 inches. The weight of the text block may tug at the hinges and cause a sag in the spine – requiring a future repair!

Temperature, Humidity and Light

Heat accelerates book and paper deterioration and for every 20°F that rate almost doubles. High humidity promotes harmful chemical reactions and when combined with warm temperatures encourages mold growth and insect activity. Extremely low relative humidity leads to desiccation and brittleness in items. Extreme fluctuations of heat and humidity are also damaging.

Books and paper are like sponges, they easily absorb and give off moisture from the air. They expand and contract along with changes in heat and humidity. When they are densely stored they can weather mild changes in heat and humidity.

Books are like wine: you want to find a consistent and balanced level of heat and moisture. A preferred stable temperature no higher than 70°F and a stable relative humidity between a minimum of 30% and a maximum of 50% is recommended.

In Seattle, a dehumidifier may be required and in New England in winter a humidifier may be required. As a general rule, don't store books anywhere you wouldn't store people.

Books are also very sensitive to light. Don't store books where direct sunlight will fall on them – over time the color will be leached from the surface. UV light also breaks down the fibers in cloth and paper. And be aware that fluorescent lights (including the new compact variety) and tungsten-halogen lights emit UV radiation that is damaging to books (although this can be offset with special UV-filtering plastic covers).

Shipping

Books that are shipped should arrive in the same condition as when they were purchased. It is not the customer's responsibility to ensure this happens Books in transit need to be protected against most things sharp, blunt or wet. Not much can protect a book from the extremes, such as being submerged or being run over by a forklift, but protection against average abuse is expected.

Inner Layers

Plastic. A polybag or even a grocery bag slipped over the bundle can save the book when left on a wet porch. A polybag will also prevent accidental damage from the packing process.

Tissue. A layer of tissue paper is a good start, especially if the skin of the book is sensitive. If you are using newsprint, begin with a polybag to prevent transfer.

Cardboard. Sandwich the book between two pieces of cardboard of a size that extends BEYOND the corners of the book covers.

Bubble wrap. Small bubble bubble wrap, the more valuable a book the more layers it deserves.

Outer Layers

Envelope. If the book bundle is small enough, you can slip it into a Jiffybag® with or without padding. Jiffybag® padding is not a guaranteed replacement for prewrapping the book, but it can suffice if the book is very small and sandwiched between cardboard.

Box or boxfold. Using brand new shipping boxes for each and every sale is not always cost effective. But if you are shipping a $$$ book to a $$$ customer, taking the time and effort to make a professional impression with a new box will encourage repeat business. Use new boxes when practical and used boxes when possible. If you are reusing a box that is still in good shape, make sure that all previous shipping labels have been peeled off and all barcodes and text have been blackened out. Do not use printed boxes; these give a very bad impression and are usually frowned on by the Post Office.

NOTE. Pack with your head as well as your hands. A $5 book doesn't need a $50 packing job. However, the $5 dollar customer is just as delighted to get an undamaged book as the $50 customer. Besides, if you KNOW you packed it properly, you won't hear "but it was damaged when it arrived."

VENDORS

SicPress.com, 14 Pleasant St., Methuen, MA 01844, www.sicpress.com sales@sicpress.com

TALAS, 568 Broadway, New York, NY 10012, 212-219-0770, talasonline.com, info@talasonline.com

Highsmith, Inc., W5527 State Road 106 - P.O. Box 800, Fort Atkinson, WI 53538-0800, 800-558-2110, highsmith.com, service@highsmith.com

University Products, P.O. Box 101 - 517 Main St.,Holyoke, MA. 01041, 800-336-4847, librarysuppliers.com,custserv@librarysuppliers.com

Bookmakers International, 8260 Patuxent Range Rd.,Jessup, Maryland 20794, 301-604-7787, www.bookmakerscatalog.com, bookmakers@earthlink.net

Brodart, P.O. Box 100, McElhattan, PA 17748, 888-820-4377, shopbrodart.com, supplies.customerservice@brodart.com

Demco, Inc., P.O. Box 7488, Madison, WI 53707-7488, 800-962-4463, demco.com, custserv@demco.com

Gaylord, P. O. Box 4901, Syracuse NY 13221-4901, 800-634-6307, gaylord.com, customerservice@gaylord.com

J. Hewitt & Sons, Kinauld Leather Works, Currie, Edinburgh, EH14 5RS Scotland, +44 (0) 131 449 2206, hewit.comsale@hewit.com

Hollinger Metal Edge, Inc., 6340 Bandini Ave.,Commerce, Ca 90040, 800-862-2228,hollingermetaledge.com, info@metaledgeinc.com

Made in the USA
Las Vegas, NV
17 February 2024

85932180R00049